Creative Writing

KINGFISHER
NEW YORK

KINGFISHER
LONDON & NEW YORK

Text and design copyright © Toucan Books Ltd. 2013
Based on an original concept by Toucan Books Ltd.
Illustrations copyright © Simon Basher 2013

Published in the United States by Kingfisher,
175 Fifth Ave., New York, NY 10010
Kingfisher is an imprint of Macmillan Children's Books, London

Consultant: Meg Rosoff
Book titles recommended by members of the Children's
Book Committee, Bank Street College of Education

Designed and created by Basher www.basherbooks.com
Text written by Mary Frances Budzik

Mary Frances Budzik dedicates this book to Caitlin, Connor, and Daniel
With thanks to Lisa Von Drasek, Jennifer M. Brown, Elizabeth Segal,
Isadora Carreras, Molly Welsh Kruger, and Linda Greengrass

Distributed in the U.S. and Canada by Macmillan,
175 Fifth Ave., New York, NY 10010

Library of Congress Cataloging-in-Publication Data has been applied for.

ISBN: 978-0-7534-7055-8

Kingfisher Books are available for special promotions and premiums.
For details contact: Special Markets Department,
Macmillan, 175 Fifth Ave., New York, NY 10010.

For more information, please visit www.kingfisherbooks.com

Printed in China
9 8 7 6 5 4 3 2
2SCHOL/1013/UTD/WKT/128MA

CONTENTS

Introduction
Creative Writing

The coolest thing about creative writing is the freedom it brings. Absolutely any idea you have for a story can be a winner—you can write it just for yourself, to figure things out in your head. But if you want an audience, your story has to be good enough for others to read, so it helps to know a few tricks of the trade. Finding the right words for brilliant brainstorms depends on more than just inspiration. As with any art, success lies in using the forms, tools, and techniques that writers have been using for centuries.

The writer Roald Dahl (1916–1990) fully embraced artistic freedom in his matter-of-fact tales of children facing bravely up to terrible trouble—often created by adults—and he never worried about being nice or comforting! He was not afraid to "drown" greedy boys like Augustus Gloop in chocolate or to announce that real witches simply live to squelch children. His plots were unique: Just when things couldn't be any more bleak for James, he is suddenly off on an adventure inside a giant rolling peach with talking insects for company! What better proof could you have that anything goes?

Roald Dahl

Chapter 1
What's the Story?

Don't worry—in this world, it's a very good thing to tell tall tales! Stories have been told since the days of cavemen sitting around campfires, waxing poetic on the mammoth that got away. Making up stories is a lot of fun, and this lively crew will help you start your yarns spinning. Known as genres, each of these literary types has its own telltale traits. Eerie Horror is just itching to give you the creeps; dreamy Fantasy cannot wait to transport you to some far-off realm; and inquisitive Mystery comes with a whole lot of clues to follow. If *you've* got a story to tell, these imaginative geniuses are sure to guide you on your way.

Adventure
■ What's the Story?

☀ A journey in which the main character (protagonist) is tested
☀ Survival depends on a character's stamina, wit, and courage
☀ Often has a symbolic object to find or a task to complete

Watch out! I have a tendency toward shipwreck! In my world, Protagonist can't even take a hike in the hills without stumbling onto a secret cavern . . . and darn if it doesn't reveal a map marked with an *X* and a drawing of a chest overflowing with doubloons—and daggers.

Of course, the directions on the map are in code—aren't they always? It'll take a sharp mind and an instinct for survival to puzzle them out. But this is no ordinary place. Just as Protagonist plans nothing more than a pleasant nap in the garden, sure enough, a wizard shows up and whisks the unfortunate away on a nerve-racking journey that takes years! But good old Pro always returns, much changed, and with the satisfaction of knowing that success in the quest has kept the world safe from harm.

Three to read:

● *My Side of the Mountain*, by Jean Craighead George (1959)
● *Island of the Blue Dolphins*, by Scott O'Dell (1960)
● *The Titanic: An Interactive History Adventure*, by Bob Temple (2008)

Adventure

Horror
■ What's the Story?

✳ A story that inspires feelings of apprehension, fear, and terror
✳ Fear is an inborn biological response in all people
✳ Many fairy tales, such as "Hansel and Gretel," are horror stories

I'll give you the chills! Let's walk in the graveyard on a moonless night! Dark and dramatic, I live for the moment when your breath is taken away—temporarily. I'm all about making the familiar strange and the eerie everywhere. Never a wholesome sort, I frequent crypts, caskets, and moldy mansions that have seen better days.

My tales are filled with shadowy forces and wailing wraiths. There's more to the ordinary than meets the eye . . . and it might just be on the other side of that dungeon door! My power to disturb isn't just for thrills, though—I can advise caution and show how the unseen has power in everyday life. Have you ever woken up and wondered where you are? Ever looked in a mirror and seen a face not your own? That would be a horror story for sure!

Three to read:
● *Bunnicula*, by Deborah and James Howe (1979)
● *Scary Stories to Tell in the Dark*, by Alvin Schwartz (1981)
● *A Tale Dark and Grimm*, by Adam Gidwitz (2010)

Horror

Science Fiction

■ What's the Story?

☀ A realistic story set in an alternative or future world
☀ Explores the incredible possibilities of science and technology
☀ *Frankenstein*, by Mary Shelley, is a great early example (1818)

I'm impatient with things as they are. Wouldn't it be cool if you had jet-powered sneakers that made you fly? Or what about if you could understand all human—and nonhuman—languages instantly?

I'm a whiz at biology, chemistry, astronomy, genetics, and the rest. They are the ingredients I use to cook up something new and different. My nonstop ingenuity keeps me working overtime to stay unreal: Scads of my once wild predictions have collided smack into ordinary reality—think communication satellites (Aldous Huxley's *Brave New World*, 1932). The places I describe are at times utopian (carefree and happy), at other times dystopian (bleak and prisonlike). I'm socially conscious—well, science often seems to be about how to comprehend life, doesn't it?

Three to read:

● *Aliens for Breakfast*, by Jonathan Etra and Stephanie Spinner (1988)
● *The City of Ember*, by Jeanne DuPrau (2003)
● *Oh No!: Or How My Science Project Destroyed the World*, by Mac Barnett (2010)

Science Fiction

Fantasy
What's the Story?

✳ Fiction set in a place where the rules of magic are in force
✳ The supernatural is beyond scientific understanding
✳ An early fantasy novel was J. M. Barrie's *Peter Pan*, 1911

I'm otherworldly. The places I frequent are not far from your familiar world, but they can be tricky to find. Protagonist may step into a wardrobe on a dark, rainy day, loiter on an abandoned train platform, or peer down a shady alley to discover an elsewhere that appears behind a puff of green smoke.

Unlike my futuristically inspired friend, Science Fiction, I tend to look back to the past. I'm not always logical—magic, after all, is an art, not a science. Falcons are able to speak; beans cast across fertile ground sprout shoots that grow into castles. The ring that Protagonist finds bestows special powers, yet there is no end to the challenges in store. This is a world in which light is threatened by dark forces that must be resisted on all accounts if Good is to prevail.

Three to read:
● *Catwings*, by Ursula K. Le Guin (1988)
● *Knights of the Kitchen Table*, by Jon Scieszka (1991)
● *The New Kid at School*, by Kate McMullan (1997)

Fantasy

Mystery
What's the Story?

* Story in which a protagonist investigates a mystery or crime
* The detective (amateur or professional) often has a sidekick
* Canny clues help connect the dots

I'm a cagey type whose world is seldom as it seems. Wary Protagonist might look for the story behind the story but, dogged by dastardly deeds, seems instead to stumble into muddles, mayhem, and even murder.

I scatter clues for detectives, private investigators, and interfering old ladies. I lead Protagonist into some sticky situations and courageous capers, but good old Pro is always equal to the challenge, refusing to back off despite ominous omens, threats from thieves, or pleas from the police. It is a question of having to be supremely self-confident, of trusting that gumption and grit will save the day. Even then, with criminals corralled and cooped up for good, it won't be long before I set yet another trail of trouble. This game of wits is just too much fun to play.

Three to read:
- *Detectives in Togas*, by Henry Winterfeld (1956)
- *Cam Jansen and the Mystery of the Stolen Diamonds*, by David A. Adler (1980)
- *Hoot*, by Carl Hiaasen (2002)

Mystery

Diary
■ What's the Story?

✳ A record of events not usually meant to be read by others
✳ In fiction, it allows a main character to tell his or her story
✳ Diaries are always written in the first person

Writing about myself is what I do, but hey, it's private, so no one's asking *you* to snoop. My plan is to wait until I get famous and then self-publish for posterity! In the old days, I'd scribble in a classic book of tooled leather guarded by a little brass lock and key. Today, though, you're more likely to find me as an online blog—password-protected, naturally!

I keep a record of daily life, warts and all! I'm writing for myself, so I don't pull any punches. If my mom or friends are getting on my nerves, it's written there in my very own words. As far as spelling and grammar go, I don't strive for perfection, but that's part of my charm. The only standards here are mine, and I don't get graded! I'm written by all kinds—from U.S. presidents to wimpy kids—everyone turns to me when they need to let off steam!

Three to read:
● *Amelia's Notebook*, by Marissa Moss (1995)
● *Diary of a Worm*, by Doreen Cronin (2003)
● *Diary of a Wimpy Kid*, by Jeff Kinney (2007)

Diary

Poetry
■ What's the Story?

✳ An experience, emotion, or idea in concentrated form
✳ Arranges words in rhythmical, frequently rhymed patterns
✳ *Poem* comes from the ancient Greek *poiein*, meaning "create"

I've got the beat, you bet. My syllables are stressed and my meters are measured. I'm a rhyming fool, a patternmaker of sounds. It all makes for rhythmic speech you can just about dance to! I'm so close to song that it can be hard to tell us apart, but while song often sings alongside an instrument, such as a piano or guitar, all I need is a voice.

Around the time of the Vikings (okay, I know I'm old), I was the main entertainment, bellowed at banquets, all one big brag of bold battle deeds. A few centuries later, I softened up and helped lovesick courtiers convince noble ladies that they really, really cared. Today, my talent for saying a lot with a little keeps me rapping at poetry slams and tweeting on Twitter. My flair for multiple meanings makes my words do double the work in half the time!

Two to read:
● *The Random House Book of Poetry for Children,* selected by Jack Prelutsky (1983)
● *Talking Like the Rain: A Read-to-Me Book of Poems,* selected by X. J. Kennedy and Dorothy M. Kennedy (1992)

Poetry

Chapter 2
Scene Setters

If writing stories is your thing, you can rely on this rock-steady crew to provide the whats and whens, the wheres and hows at the heart of the matter! Sure, Setting does most of the work—after all, a story's not a story until it's got a happening place to call its own—but what about the rest of the gang? Well, tone-setting Title provides a catchy name to draw you in, while whimsical Atmosphere drifts around the place creating just the right mood. It may take a while to find Theme, but dig deep, and the dude will be there, right at the foundation of a good story, all set to get the message across.

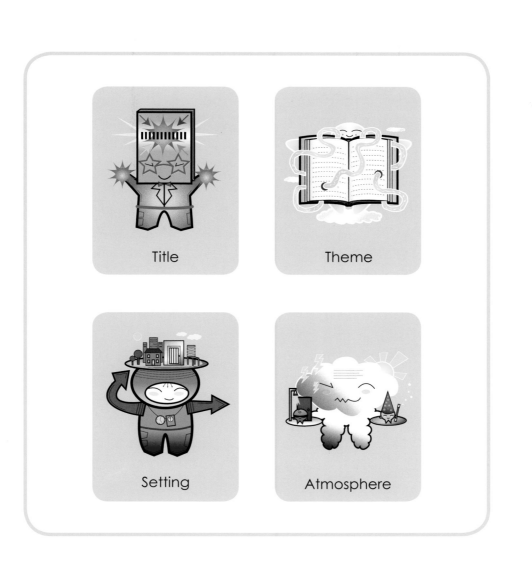

Title

Theme

Setting

Atmosphere

Title
■ Scene Setters

☀ The name by which a book, a story, or a poem is known
☀ Usually the first impression a potential reader has of a book
☀ Written in a tone to match the story: funny, mysterious, sad

Lookin' good! No story with self-respect, no poem with panache, no mystery with mojo wants to leave the library without a title that toots a horn! A moniker that makes waves! Why pick a ho-hum handle, a lackluster label, when I can give you something that makes the other books on the shelf step back?

Get the picture? Well, I'm not exactly a retiring sort. I'm out there working the crowd, glad-handing readers right and left—after all, I am the first thing they see when they scan a crowded bookshelf. I wear my name on a book's spine with pride, and it doesn't end there. It's my job to give potential readers clues about the style, theme, and plot of a book. I'm there to tell them—loud and clear—that they've found just the story they've been searching for.

Try these:
- Think of a title for a science-fiction story, for a mystery, and for an adventure.
- Chapter titles within a story often have the same tone and/or format. Outline the plot for a story by making up three chapter titles that are similar in style.

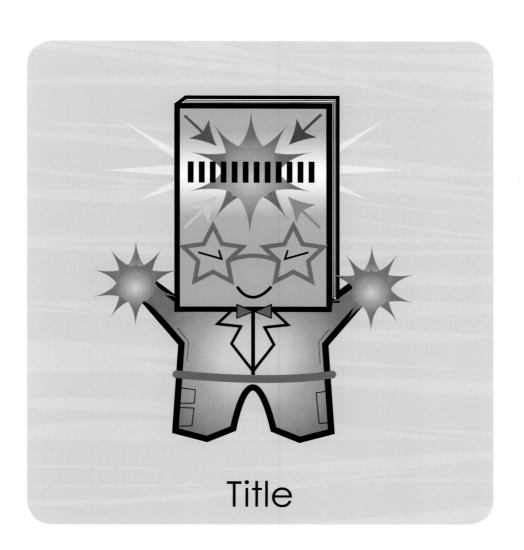

Title

Theme
Scene Setters

✳ A central message or idea expressed by a story or poem
✳ Usually woven into a story rather than stated outright
✳ Often has a significance beyond the story itself

I'm a thoughtful type and sometimes a bit shy. Sure, Plot likes to scurry here and there, Plot Device teases readers with its tricks, and colorful Figurative Language draws all eyes. Meanwhile, I meditate peacefully at the very center of a story, waiting patiently for you to find me.

I often speak through other elements of a story rather than in a voice of my own, which means I can be a little hard to spot. I am worth seeking out, though. If you pay close attention and, like me, practice quiet reflection, you will hear my message, I'm sure—I'm intuitive! Ask yourself: Are there subjects in the story that reappear in different ways in different episodes? What makes Protagonist especially happy or sad? Does the story's title offer any clues? Before you know it, you'll have found me!

Try these:
● Identify the different themes in your favorite novel.
● Choose a simple theme (for example, "Friends are found in unexpected places"), then work on a story to illustrate the theme.

Theme

Setting
■ Scene Setters

❋ The physical and historical location of a story
❋ A combination of time, place, and cultural environment
❋ Important to the plot of genres such as adventure and mystery

Come in, come in. Set your storytelling baggage down and unpack. Get comfortable and take a good look around you. My place is your place . . .

I'm full of gossip—about the house, the history of the place, the terrain, the weather, and even the time of day. With me as your guide, you're sure to notice the scenery. But I'm not simply a convenient place in which the action happens. I direct attention to those important little details that really shouldn't be missed. I can hide Mystery's clues or help create Atmosphere. At times I can symbolize values so powerful—say, a home that stands for security or family history—that Character will die to defend me. Other times that lightweight can't flee me fast enough (such as when I'm a dungeon or a dragon's lair)!

Try these:
● Describe the perfect setting for a horror story or a fantasy set in the past.
● The setting can give clues to the theme of a story—for example, a story set in a desert can suggest a theme of loneliness. Think of two more examples.

Setting

Atmosphere
■ Scene Setters

✳ A mood in the setting or in a character's frame of mind
✳ A change in atmosphere can signal a shift in the plot
✳ Expressed by choice of words, setting, and descriptive details

When I visit Setting, you can feel something in the air. That show-off is little more than a bare stage without me! And when I buddy up with Viewpoint—ooooh, the possibilities!

You see, I like to mirror Viewpoint's feelings and have the power to change Character's mood. If I'm feeling eerie, the sky darkens, stars snuff out, tree branches grow claws, crows caw, and a cold wind kicks up. That someone loitering on a doorstep is a stranger huddling deep inside a hooded cape. But get me in a fantasy mood, and it's a different story. The sky glimmers with an unusual green glow, stars shimmer, trees talk, and crows become messengers, carried by the whispering wind. This time, the stranger is a wizard, witch, or warlock who appears in a shower of multicolored sparks.

Try these:
- Write the opening scene for a story so that it sets the mood for what follows.
- Describe how a character such as a witch or a pirate can create the atmosphere for a story. Use a character in a story you know to help you.

Atmosphere

Chapter 3
Schemers and Dreamers

When it comes to writing a gripping tale, you'll not get far without the Schemers and Dreamers. First off, there's the ideas guy, Plot, who decides what a story is all about, who stars in it, and what happens. Ever practical, Structure is then at hand to arrange Plot's events in an order that works—after all, you have to get from the beginning of your story to the end somehow. Flashback and Flash-forward appear from time to time, while Plot Device throws in the occasional red herring. Despite missing most of the action, Denouement steps in right at the end to provide a welcome return to normality.

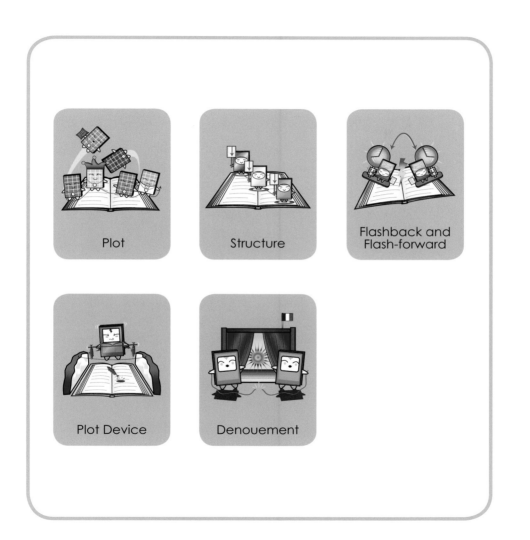

Plot

Structure

Flashback and Flash-forward

Plot Device

Denouement

Plot
■ Schemers and Dreamers

✳ A sequence of events that tells a complete story
✳ Depends on movement through time for its development
✳ Can move around between present, past, and future time

I'm the big boss—nobody moves without my say-so! Master of everyone's fate, it's up to me whether Character has a school day or a snow day, and I know exactly what lies at the bottom of the lake when a kid dives off the raft.

Whether I pick and choose events to express a grand idea or let chaos reign just for laughs, a story is nothing without me. I'm always laying plans, tugging people and events this way and that. I'm a bit of a practical joker—after all, my motive is to create conflict; that's what makes a story interesting. Just when you think things are all set, *boom*, I'll send a ferocious dog across your path in what's known as a plot twist. Or, like a mad chemist, I'll brew up a side story (subplot). I'll let it bubble along on its own or toss it into the main plot to see what explodes!

Try these:

● Write down some starter plot ideas, using just a sentence for each. For example, Tom Harper has a guilty secret; Sally is drawn to a strange glow on the horizon.
● Next, think of a plot twist that would make each story more interesting.

Plot

Structure
■ Schemers and Dreamers

☀ The arrangement of the events within a plot
☀ Gives a story a beginning, a middle, and an end
☀ Getting the order of events just so increases a story's impact

I am Plot's conscience. Addicted to the roller-coaster ride of events, Plot has a tendency to overwhelm a story like a tsunami, scattering mishap and misfortune all around. Well, it's my job to make Plot stop and think.

I show that hothead some restraint! Yes, with me onboard, Plot chooses balance over bedlam and cause over coincidence. You see, I have a set of tools that help organize events in a logical progression, each incident causing the next. Thus Plot is able to set the scene (exposition), get things moving (rising action), stir things up (conflict), put on the brakes (suspense), cue the thunder (climax), and let everything settle back to earth (denouement). If I've done my job well, you'll feel like everything that happened was meant to be!

Try these:
- See if you can find the exposition, rising action, conflict, climax, and denouement in your favorite book.
- Can you reorder some of the events without altering the outcome of the story?

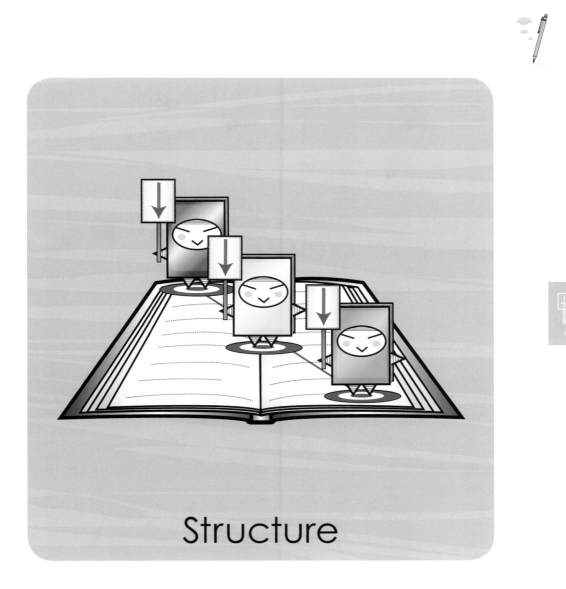

Structure

Flashback and Flash-forward

Schemers and Dreamers

* Scenes that take a reader backward or forward in time
* Reveals something important about the plot or its characters
* Often told as a story within a story

Wouldn't you just love to be us? We've got the coolest job in creative writing: time travel! With our help, getting lost in a story takes on a whole new meaning.

A nod from one of us and you're suddenly someplace else—zapped to that back-in-the-past or forward-to-the-future time and place that puts the here and now in context. With us around, the present is only one small part of the story; the wider your perspective, the more you understand. Or maybe not! Though the scenes we conjure up often unravel Plot's twisted knots, sometimes (depending on how sly the author is) they simply add a new kink! Welcome to the labyrinth!

Try these:

● Write down three ideas for a flashback or flash-forward within a story.
● Write a story scene in which a character remembers as a flashback something that has happened to him or her.

Flashback and
Flash-forward

Plot Device
Schemers and Dreamers

☀ A storytelling technique that adds suspense to a plot
☀ Examples include red herrings and cliff-hangers
☀ Plot twists often bring an unexpected conclusion to a story

When Plot is feeling weak and run-down, like it's losing its grip (on the audience, that is), I am always ready to come to the rescue. There's nothing I like more than a good rummage through my cupboards. They are simply stuffed with remedies for a sagging story line.

Believe me, my tricks are highly effective. Take red herring—a tantalizing false clue that fools careless readers into thinking they've got everything figured out, only to be outsmarted by a powerful plot twist later on! Then there's teasing cliff-hanger, who tightens the tension by saying "to be continued" just as the door to the secret room is about to creak open. For sure, the temptation to overdo it is always there, but if I'm smart, I can keep readers frantically focused right up to Plot's grand finale!

Try these:
- Write an exciting story that ends on a cliff-hanger.
- Think of a plot in which a red herring leads a private investigator to suspect the wrong person.

Plot Device

Denouement

■ Schemers and Dreamers

✴ The unraveling of the main dramatic complications in a story
✴ May solve a crisis, but the solution is not always a happy one
✴ In a book series, it can foreshadow the plot of the next book

So, the usual cast of characters, including Protagonist and Antagonist, have had their fun or done their worst. Plot's crisis may be over now, but there are consequences to face and it's time for me to step in.

My awesome French name (pronounced *day-nu-mon*) means "unravel the knot." And that's exactly what I do: I reveal mistaken identities, break up mismatched mates, and extract neat confessions. I provide an all-important breathing space for the reader to reflect on what's happened and what it all means. I resolve issues, that's for certain, but it doesn't mean that I can put everything back the way it was. There will doubtless be a few grazed knees and battered egos, but at least I will have restored calm . . . well, for the time being.

Try these:
- Choose one of your favorite stories and describe the denouement.
- Think of a simple plot for a mystery—say, something goes missing. Write a denouement for the story, describing how that thing is found again.

Denouement

Chapter 4
Heroes and Villains

Here's a fine bunch of rampaging rascals—the good guys, the bad guys, and the spinners of fine yarns. What form will Character take from one tale to the next? How will Protagonist fare, tirelessly going eyeball to eyeball with opponent Antagonist, seemingly against all odds? You'll have to ask Viewpoint, of course, storyteller and narrator extraordinaire. For Viewpoint is always in control of a story. That's right! When it comes to spilling the beans, Viewpoint decides exactly what it is that you should or should not know. What you have to decide is whether or not to believe what you are reading . . .

Character

Protagonist

Antagonist

Viewpoint

First Person

Third Person

Character
■ Heroes and Villains

* ☀ An individual who has a role in a story
* ☀ Could be an animal, ghost, or monster, as well as a person
* ☀ Defined by appearance, behavior, personal history, habits

Poor me! I rattle around inside Setting while Plot's twists and turns come at me from all sides. I need development pronto or I won't get any respect: No one will believe in me.

Depending on the role I play, I can be flat or round. No, that does not mean I get squished or stuffed. If I'm flat, I'm known for one personality trait that just about takes over my life. If I'm round, I've got a complex nature that makes me do things that take you by surprise. Pretty simple so far, but there's more: I can also be static or dynamic. Static, and I stay the same no matter what Plot throws at me. Dynamic, though, and I've got some changing to do. That's where the author comes in, because he or she has to decide how and why that change will happen. Well, nobody said character building was easy, did they?

Try these:
* ● Stock characters conform to a common "type," such as the evil stepmother. Can you think of three more?
* ● Think about some characters in the books you've read. Are they flat or round?

Character

Protagonist
■ Heroes and Villains

✳ The main character; the one with whom the reader identifies
✳ Name comes from the Greek for "leading person in a contest"
✳ Does not always have to be good, like a hero or heroine

I have a magnetism that I just cannot seem to shake. I am the focus of all eyes, even when I don't want to be, and especially when I start to draw Antagonist's attention. Still, it's my destiny to rise to the challenge. I may not look like anything special, but I am noble, because I never give up. Courage lurks deep in my heart, and just as I stumble into Plot's perils, it shows its face.

Protagonist

Try these:

● Write a short story that is narrated by the protagonist.
● An antihero is a protagonist without the traditional positive heroic qualities. List three you've come across in the books that you have read.

Antagonist
Heroes and Villains

* The character or force that works against a protagonist
* Name comes from the Greek for "opponent, enemy, or rival"
* Not necessarily bad—can be complex, even sympathetic

Antagonist

There's nothing like a little stress and strife to keep Protagonist alert, and that's where I come in. My selfless commitment to conflict allows old Pro to be noble—to do the right thing. And me? Famous for being rotten, I'm booed even by the back rows! Yet, without me, life would be dull, dull, dull. I keep everyone on the edge of their seat. I move the story forward, man!

Try these:

● Rewrite your story from the opposite page with the antagonist as your narrator.
● Try writing a short story in which your antagonist is a force, such as poverty, disease, or the weather.

Viewpoint

■ Heroes and Villains

✳ The perspective from which a story is told
✳ Usually given through the eyes and voice of a narrator
✳ An unreliable narrator is one that tries to mislead the reader

Does a story exist if there's no one to tell it? I'm here, with my pals First Person and Third Person, to make sure you never have to discover the answer to that question!

Getting inside Character's head is what I'm about— and as soon as I do, I start tattling about the view. My loyalty is to the story and the best way to tell it. What you see and hear totally depends on me—I, alone, decide what's important. Let's get things into perspective for a moment: I may know it *all*, but how much should I let *you* know? For example, I might choose to tell you what every character in the story sees, or I might settle on just one of them. The scope of my story may be far and wide or near and narrow. I might conceal certain facts from you or even fib a little—well, it has been known to happen!

Try this:

● Choose your favorite fairy tale and write it from three different viewpoints. For example, you could rewrite "Little Red Riding Hood" from the girl's viewpoint, from her grandmother's, and from that of the wolf.

Viewpoint

First Person
■ Heroes and Villains

- ☀ An "I" who narrates a story, typically the main character
- ☀ Can be the voice of an animal as well as a person
- ☀ Perspective seldom switches to another character in the story

Welcome to my own private world. I've got a tale to tell and I want to share it with you. It's a story so close to my heart that I'm the only one who can tell it the way it needs to be told. I want it to sound just so, in my tone of voice and my words— no one else's. And when you listen, you won't be outside my story looking in. You will be right there, experiencing it with me.

First Person

Try these:

- ● Write a short story in the first person from the perspective of an animal.
- ● Create a character based on someone famous and try writing a day-in-the-life diary using the first person.

Third Person
Heroes and Villains

* A narrator who tells a story using "he," "she," "it," or "they"
* Can express the viewpoint of all the characters in a story
* Not usually one of the characters in the story

Third Person

Hey, there's a big world of characters out there with enough viewpoints to make anyone dizzy! That's where I come in. With a welcome lack of bias, I tell a story while staying out of it myself! The characters simply lend me their ears, their eyes, their feelings, and their thoughts. Mine is a world seen from every angle—I will even let you know what's happening behind the scenes!

Try these:

● Rewrite your first-person story from the opposite page in the third person.
● Write a story about a bunch of kids, in which each event is described using the viewpoint of a different character.

53

Chapter 5
Wordsmiths

"Smiths" are makers of tools, and these wordy characters certainly live up to their name. They are the true artisans of the storytelling world: masters of wordplay who pick and choose just the right way to say something. Blessed with a most vivid imagination, Figurative Language brings a story to life with its infinite supply of colorful imagery. Diction tinkers, taps, and tests words until they have just the right tone and timbre. To keep egos in check within this temperamental trio, Dialogue always knows just what to say. And by the time that talkative type has finished, this book will have drawn to a close.

Figurative
Language

Diction

Dialogue

Figurative Language
■ Wordsmiths

☀ The use of imagery to enhance the telling of a story
☀ Can help summon a mental picture or a sound, taste, or smell
☀ Examples include metaphors, similes, and onomatopoeia

My phrases are bells ringing through the crisp winter air. I flaunt my skill with language like a jeweled fan that I unfurl to dazzle and delight. I pluck images from my imagination like ripe purple berries from a bush.

But wait! I have many guises besides these clever comparisons. I use onomatopoeia, alliteration, and hyperbole, too. The trick is knowing how to spot them, since my words whisper and whoosh in my ear before I whoop them aloud far and wide. I jingle expressions in my pocket like loose change that I can't wait to spend on poems for a penny, novels for a nickel, fantasy for a farthing, and plays for a pound. My sentences are simply stupendous! No, you don't get plain talk when I'm around. I'm a true poet: take my word for it!

Try these:
● Reread the text and use the glossary at the end of the book to find the examples of metaphor, simile, onomatopoeia, alliteration, and hyperbole.
● Have fun writing some examples of your own.

Figurative Language

Diction
■ Wordsmiths

✳ An author's choice of words for creating different effects
✳ Depends on the purpose, the audience, and the occasion
✳ Can be formal, slang, everyday speech, or poetic

I refuse to leave the house until I'm wearing just the right words. Yep, that's right, I'm a snappy dresser. Or perhaps I should go formal and say that my preference is to select a stylish verbal ensemble? Either way, my closet is crammed with just the right phrases for every occasion.

When I choose words, I want them to express my mood exactly! Should I walk to school this morning? Yawn. I'd barely get down the driveway with those droopy duds—there's simply no energy there! No, today I'm feeling cool, casual, and I've got plenty of time, so I'll stroll to school. Wait, should I amble? Maybe I should saunter! Sashay? (I am a bit of a show-off.) Hmmm. I've been tossing terms out of my closet right and left—now I'll be late . . . or tardy, as my teacher would say.

Try this:

● "Slight" and "scrawny" both mean "thin," but the first suggests fragility and the second suggests undernourished. Think of five other pairings that have the same meaning but suggest different things—for example, "right" and "true."

Diction

Dialogue
■ Wordsmiths

✳ Conversation spoken between characters
✳ Can help show what characters are really like
✳ Uses tags, such as "he said," "she sobbed," "they chortled"

You can't shut me up! I'll natter with friends, exchange insults with enemies, and do my darnedest to engage alien life forms in meaningful conversation. Yes indeed, garrulous gabfests are my gig!

With me around, Character can't say a word without revealing something important—even if it's a lie! I can tell you where someone is from (through pronunciation and word choice). I can let you know what a person is thinking (by letting something slip out by mistake). And I can tell you more about a guy's personality (by rushing through words breathlessly for a chatty type or stammering and stuttering for a person who's shy). I dramatize events through important conversations, allowing Viewpoint to take a well-earned rest. Let's face it, talk is tops!

Try these:
● Try writing a conversation in dialect.
● Use dialogue to describe the moment a couple of kids find a stranger in their home. Think carefully about the tags and how they can add to the action.

Dialogue

Glossary

Alliteration The use of repeated consonant sounds at the beginning of words in a sequence to create energy in a phrase; for example, "the daring dog darted through the fire."

Climax The point in a story at which events and emotions (fear, anger, hope, and so forth) are at their peak. After the climax, the plot takes a turn—for better or for worse.

Conflict A struggle between characters, or between opposing forces (e.g. weather, poverty, society) that causes the characters to react, thus driving the plot forward.

Dialect A way of talking marked by unusual word choices, expressions, and accent, usually common to characters from a particular geographic region.

Foreshadow An event, symbol, or conversation that happens early in a story and that gives clues about what will come later.

Genre A word used to classify different types of literature. (From the French meaning "type.")

Hyperbole The use of deliberate exaggeration to emphasize a point; calling something ordinary "awesome," for example.

Metaphor A creative comparison that makes a connection between two unrelated things without using "like" or "as"; for example, "She is my rock."

Meter Used in poetry, words arranged to create a repeated, rhythmic pattern of stressed syllables that contributes to the effect of a poem.

Narrator The voice that tells a story. Can be a character in the story or an anonymous, all-knowing voice that does not belong to a person in the story.

Onomatopoeia A word that sounds and looks like the sound it represents: "swish," for example.

Perspective A particular point of view; in a story, we depend on the narrator's perspective for the information that we receive about the characters and events that take place.

Plot twist An unanticipated, surprising event that takes the story's action in a new or unexpected direction.

Simile Like metaphor, a simile makes a comparison but uses "like" or "as." For example, "She ran like the wind."

Slang Informal, made-up words or expressions, often originating in a particular age group or profession. Slang sometimes becomes common and thus part of standard vocabulary.

Subplot A less important story that occurs alongside the main plot and that often serves as a contrast or commentary on the main plot.

Supernatural Something that cannot be explained rationally and goes beyond the logical, scientific rules of accepted reality.

Suspense Tension created by the plot; when readers are "on the edge of their seats" to know what happens next!

Syllable The sound units that a word is broken into when correctly pronounced.

Tone The feeling (serious, silly, sorrowful, joyful) that a literary work communicates to the reader as a result of the author's attitude toward the story and characters as expressed through the way the story is told.

Wordplay Clever use of words that takes advantage of their sounds and definitions to suggest double meanings.

Index

Character entries are **bold**